EXCLUSIVELY DISTRIBUTED BY

# HAL•LEONARD®

Printed in USA.

ISBN-13: 978-0-7390-7594-4

Direct Management Group, Inc./Bradford Cobb, Martin Kirkup & Steve Jensen
Photography: Will Cotton; Original Painting by Will Cotton, Courtesy of Mary Boone Gallery
Album Art Direction: Jo Ratcliffe; Album Design: An Art Service

# C●NTENTS

# TEENAGE DREAM

Words and Music by
KATY PERRY, LUKASZ GOTTWALD,
MAX MARTIN, BENJAMIN LEVIN
and BONNIE MCKEE

**Verse 1:**

1. You think I'm pret-ty with-out an-y make-up on.___ You think I'm fun-ny, when

I tell the punch_ line wrong.___ I know you get me, so I let my walls_ come down,___

___ down._____

**Verses 2 & 3:**

2. Be - fore you met me,
3. We drove to Cal - i

Ebmaj9   Gm7   Fsus   Ebmaj9   Gm7

hands on__ me in my skin - tight__ jeans, be your teen - age__ dream to - night.__

Fsus   Ebmaj9   Gm7   Fsus

*mp*

*Chorus:*

Ebmaj9   Gm7   Fsus   Ebmaj9   Gm7

You make__ me

You_____ make me...__

*mf*

Fsus   Ebmaj9   Gm7   Fsus

feel like I'm liv - ing a teen - age__ dream, the way you turn me on.

*Bridge:*

heart rac - ing in my skin - tight jeans, be your teen - age dream to-night.

Let you put your hands on me in my skin - tight jeans, be your

teen - age dream to - night.

# LAST FRIDAY NIGHT

## (T.G.I.F.)

Words and Music by
KATY PERRY, LUKASZ GOTTWALD,
MAX MARTIN, BENJAMIN LEVIN
and BONNIE MCKEE

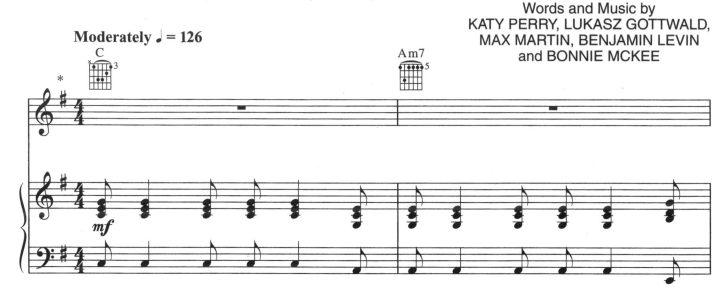

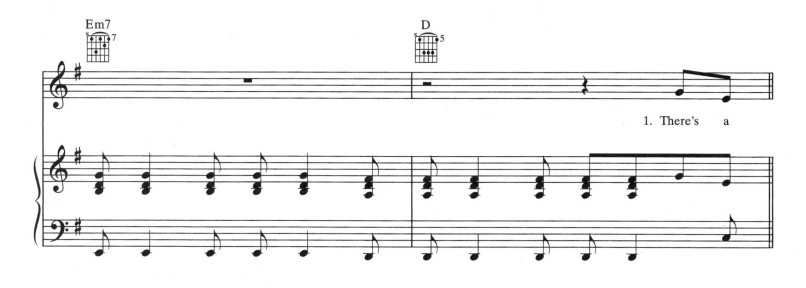

*Verse:*

*Recorded in F♯ major.

Last Friday Night - 7 - 1

all o - ver the room.___ Pink fla - min - gos in the pool.___ I smell
cit - y towed my car.___ Chan - de - lier is on the floor.___ Ripped my

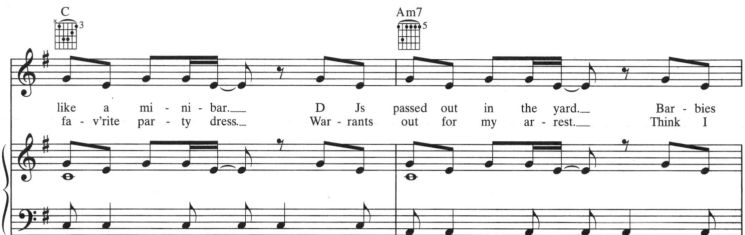

like a mi - ni - bar.___ D Js passed out in the yard.___ Bar - bies
fa - v'rite par - ty dress.___ War - rants out for my ar - rest.___ Think I

on the bar - be - cue.___ This a hick - ey or a bruise? } Pic - tures
need a gin - ger - ale.___ That was such an ep - ic fail. }

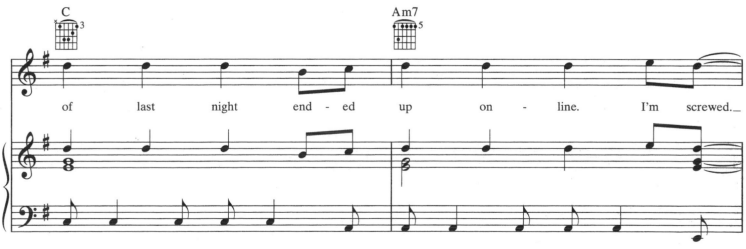

of last night end - ed up on - line. I'm screwed.___

do it all\_\_\_ a - gain.\_\_\_

1.

2. Try - ing

2.

This Fri - day night.\_\_\_ T. G. I. F.

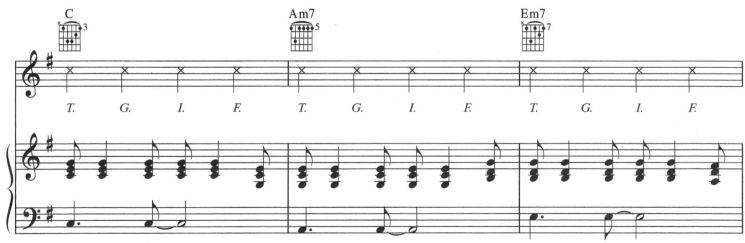

T. G. I. F. T. G. I. F. T. G. I. F.

T. G. I. F. T. G. I. F. T. G. I. F.

# CALIFORNIA GURLS

Words and Music by
KATY PERRY, LUKASZ GOTTWALD,
MAX MARTIN, BONNIE MCKEE,
BENJAMIN LEVIN and CALVIN BROADUS

California Gurls - 6 - 1

*Verses 2 & 3:*

2. Sip - pin'___ gin and juice,___ lay - ing un - der-neath the palm trees
3. Sex on the beach.___ We don't mind sand in our sti - let - tos.

(un - done.___) The boys___ break their necks___ trying to
We freak___ in my Jeep,___ Snoop Dog - gy

creep a lit - tle sneak peek (at us.___) } You could trav - el the world,___
Dogg on the ste - re - o. (Oh oh.___) } *(Sing harmony vocal 2nd time only)*

**Snoop:** *California girls, man.*

for - nia___ girls.___ Cal - i - for - nia,___

Cal - i - for - nia___ girls.___ *(Synth.)* N.C.

*Snoop rap:*
*Toned, tan,*
*Fit and ready.*
*Turn it up 'cause it's getting heavy.*
*Wild, wild West Coast,*
*These are the girls I love the most.*
*I mean the ones,*
*I mean, like she's the one.*
*Kiss her, touch her, squeeze her buns.*

*The girl's a freak,*
*She drive a Jeep,*
*And live on the beach.*
*I'm okay, I won't play.*
*I love the bait,*
*Just like I love LA.*
*Venice Beach and Palm Springs,*
*Summertime is everything.*

*Homeboys bangin' out.*
*All that a\*\* hangin' out.*
*Bikinis, zucchinis, martinis,*
*No weenies,*
*Just a king and a queenie.*
*Katy, my lady. (Yeah.)*
*Lookie here, baby.*
*I'm all up on ya,*
*'Cause you're representin' California.*
*(To Chorus:)*

# FIREWORK

Words and Music by
KATY PERRY, MIKKEL ERIKSEN,
TOR ERIK HERMANSEN,
SANDY WILHELM and ESTER DEAN

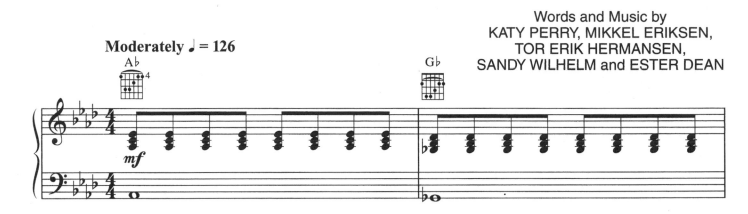

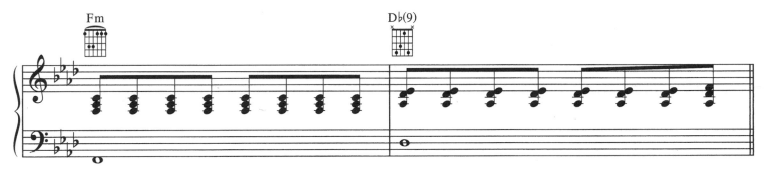

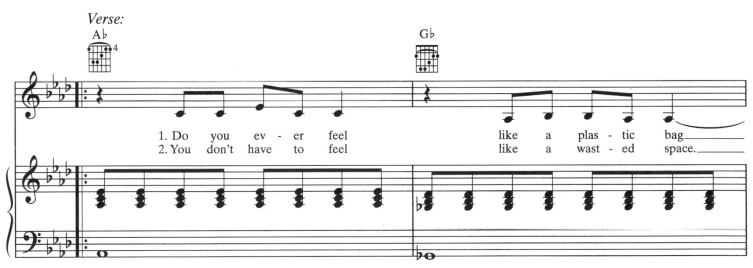

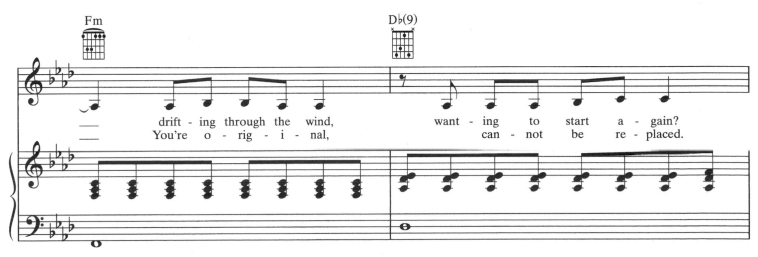

Firework - 6 - 1

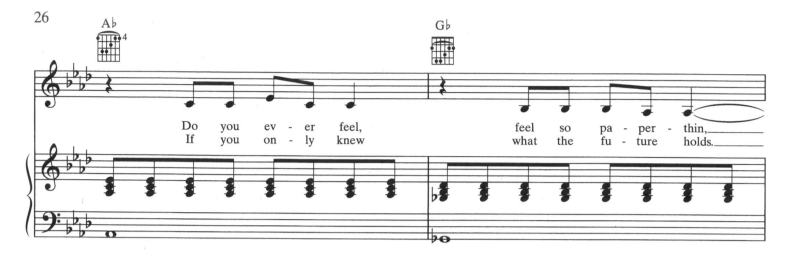

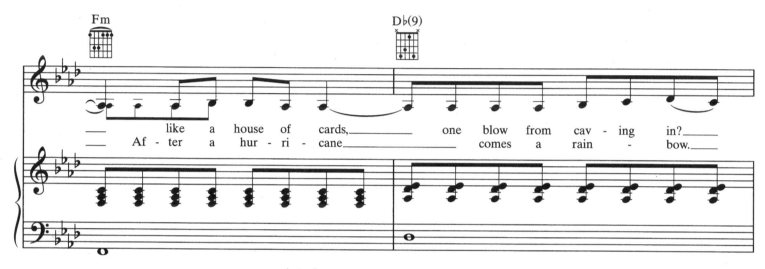

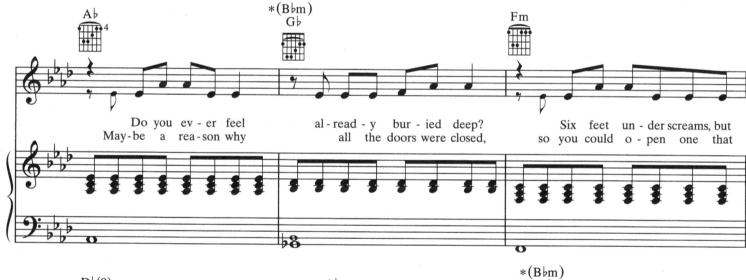

*Play B♭m chord 2nd time.

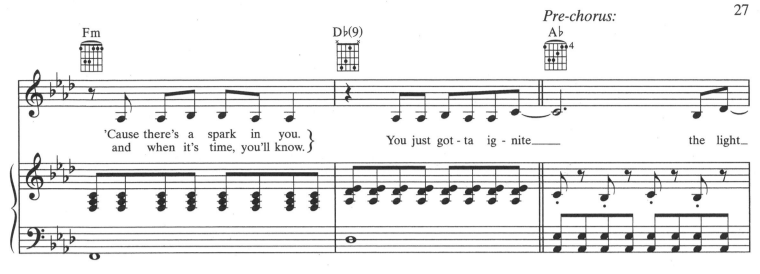

'Cause there's a spark in you.
and when it's time, you'll know.

You just got-ta ig - nite___ the light___

Pre-chorus:

___ and let_____ it shine.___ Just own___

*sim.*

___ the night___ like the Fourth_____ of___ Ju - ly.___

Chorus:

___ 'Cause, ba - by, you're a fi - re - work.___ Come on, show 'em

*cresc.*

# PEACOCK

Words and Music by
KATY PERRY, MIKKEL ERIKSEN,
TOR ERIK HERMANSEN and ESTER DEAN

**Up-tempo dance beat** ♩ = 138

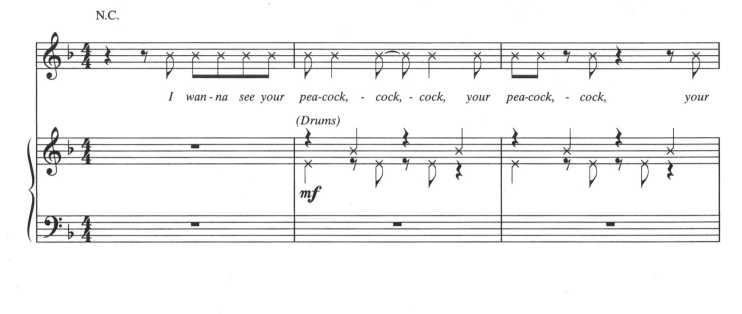

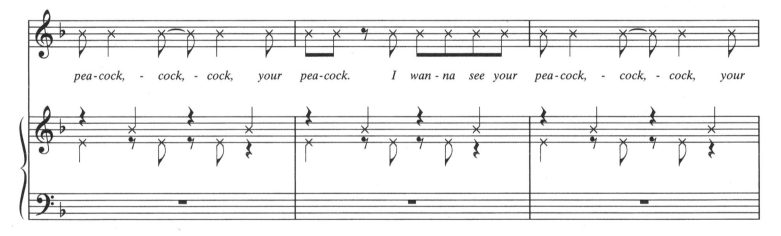

Peacock - 9 - 1

*Verse 1:*

1. Word on the street, you got some-thing to show me, me, mag-i-cal, col-or-ful, Mis-ter Mys-ter-y. I'm in-trigued for a peek, heard it's fas-ci-nat-ing.

*Come on, ba-by, let me see what you hid-ing un-der-neath.*

*Verses 2 & 3:*

2. What's up your sleeve? Such a tease; wan-na see the show in 3-D, a mov-
3. Skip the talk, heard it all, time to walk the walk. Break me off, if you

pea-cock, - cock, your pea-cock, - cock, - cock, your pea-cock. I wan-na see it.

**2.**

pea-cock, - cock, your pea-cock, - cock, - cock, your pea-cock, - cock.

*Bridge:*

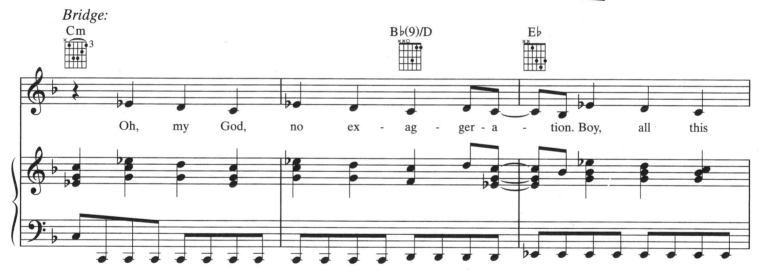

Oh, my God, no ex - ag - ger - a - tion. Boy, all this

time was worth the wait - ing. I just shed a tear.

I am so un-pre-pared. You got the

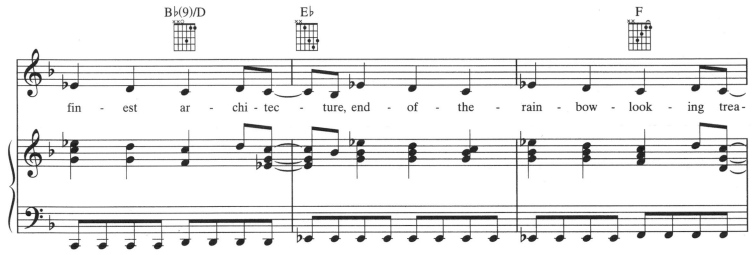

fin-est ar-chi-tec-ture, end-of-the rain-bow-look-ing trea-

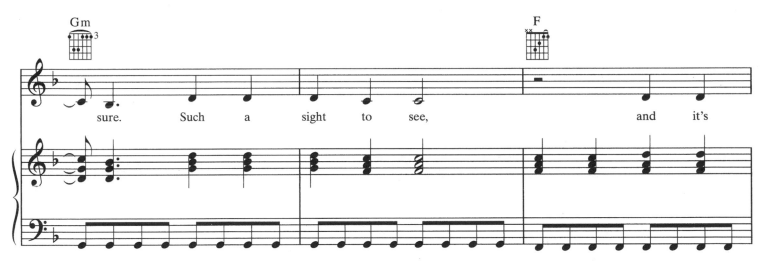

sure. Such a sight to see, and it's

*Chorus:*

all for me. Are you brave e-nough to let me see your pea-cock?

Don't be a chick-en, boy; stop act-ing like a bee-otch. I'm - a peace out if you

don't give me the pay - off. Come on, ba - by, let me see___ what you hid-ing un-der-neath.

Are you brave e - nough to let me see your pea - cock? What-cha wait-in' for? It's

time for you to show it off. Don't be a shy kind of guy. I bet it's beau - ti - ful.

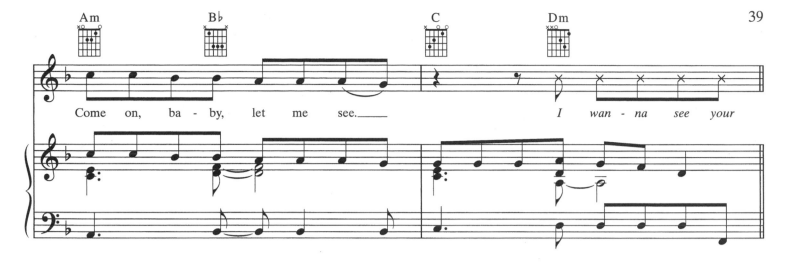

Come on, ba - by, let me see.____ I wan - na see your

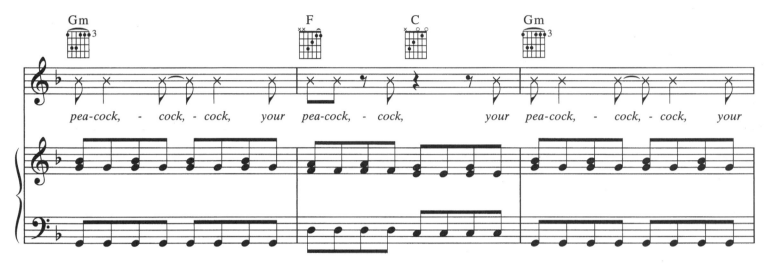

pea-cock, - cock, - cock, your pea-cock, - cock, your pea-cock, - cock, - cock, your

pea-cock. I wan - na see your pea-cock, - cock, - cock, your pea-cock, - cock.

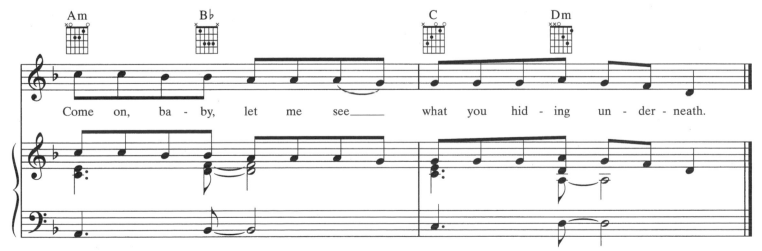

Come on, ba - by, let me see____ what you hid - ing un - der - neath.

# CIRCLE THE DRAIN

Words and Music by
KATY PERRY, CHRISTOPHER STEWART
and MONTE NEUBLE

*Recorded in E♭ minor.

Circle the Drain - 7 - 1

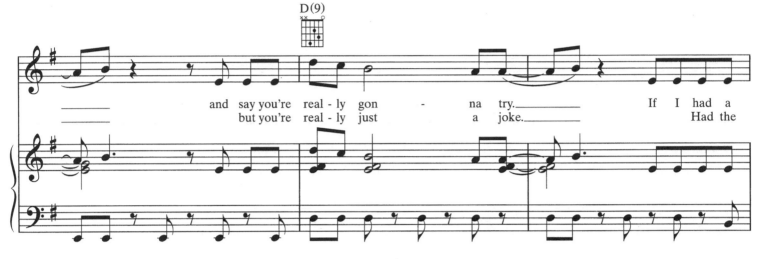

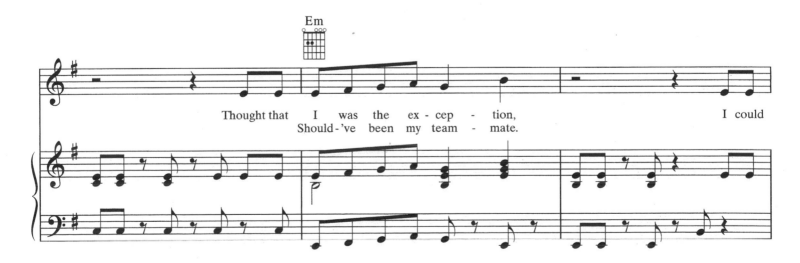

2. You say it ___

46

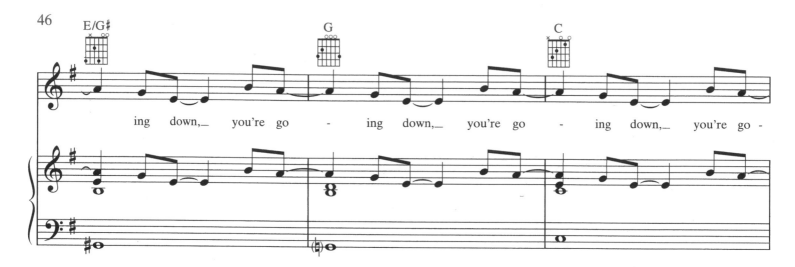

ing down,\_ you're go - ing down,\_ you're go - ing down,\_ you're go -

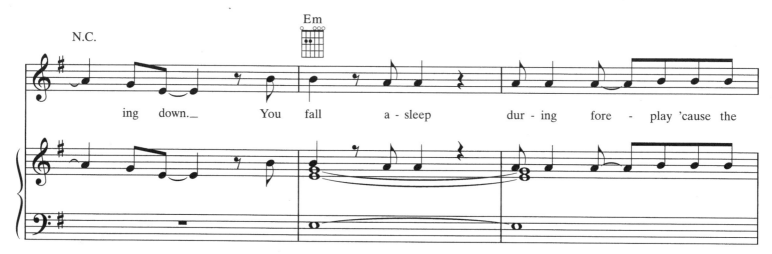

ing down.\_ You fall a - sleep dur - ing fore - play 'cause the

pills you take are more your for - té. I'm not stick - ing a - round\_

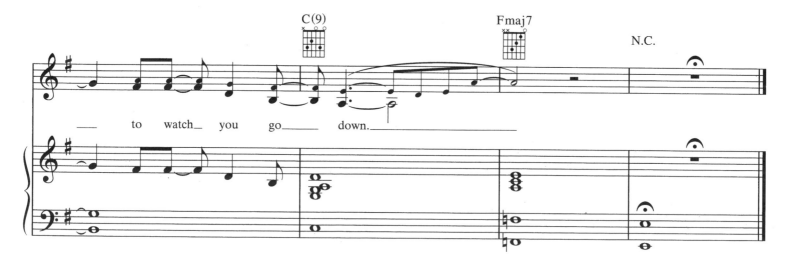

\_ to watch\_ you go\_\_\_ down._____

# THE ONE THAT GOT AWAY

Words and Music by
KATY PERRY, LUKASZ GOTTWALD
and MAX MARTIN

**Bright rock beat** ♩ = 138

*Verse 1:*

1. Sum - mer af - ter high school, when we first met,___ we'd make out in your Mus - tang to Ra - di - o - head.___ And on my eigh - teenth birth - day, we got match - ing tat - toos.___ Used to

*The One That Got Away - 7 - 1*

*To Coda*

*Bridge:*

the one,_____ the one that got a-way.

All this mon-ey can't buy me a time__ ma - chine,_____ no._____

_____ Can't re-place you with a mil - lion__ rings,_____ no._____

_____ I should have told__ you what you meant to__ me,_____ whoa,_____

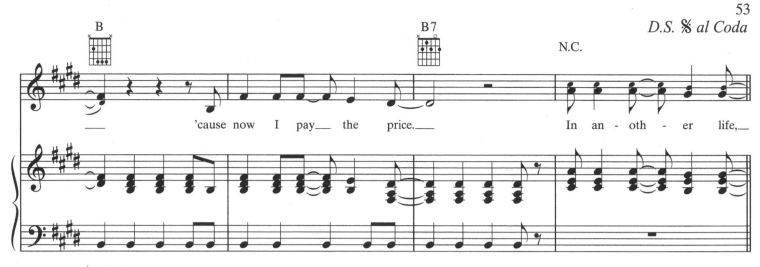

'cause now I pay___ the price.___ In an - oth - er life,___

one._____ In an - oth - er life,___

I would make___ you stay,___ so I don't have___ to say___ you were___ the one___

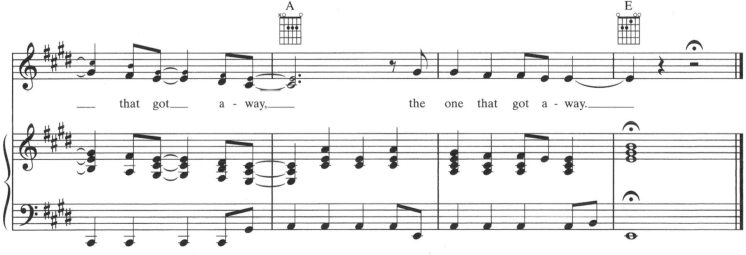

___ that got___ a - way,___ the one that got a - way.___

# E.T.

Words and Music by
KATY PERRY, LUKASZ GOTTWALD,
MAX MARTIN and JOSH COLEMAN

E.T. - 5 - 1

Take me, ta-ta-take me. Wan-na be your vic-tim, read-y for ab-duc-tion.

Boy, you're an a-li-en,___ your touch, so for-eign.___ It's su-per-nat-u-ral,___

*To Coda* ⊕

1.
___ ex - tra - ter - res - tri - al.___

2.                                    *Bridge:*
___ ex - tra - ter - res - tri - al.___ This is tran - scen - den - tal,

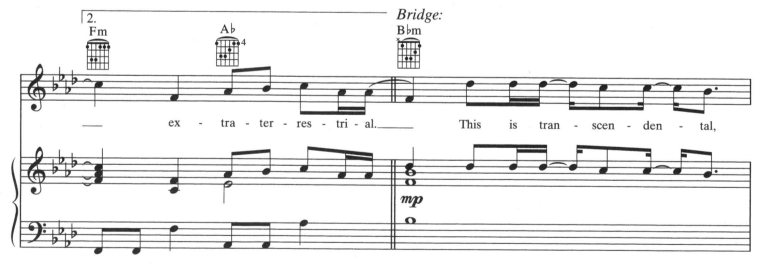

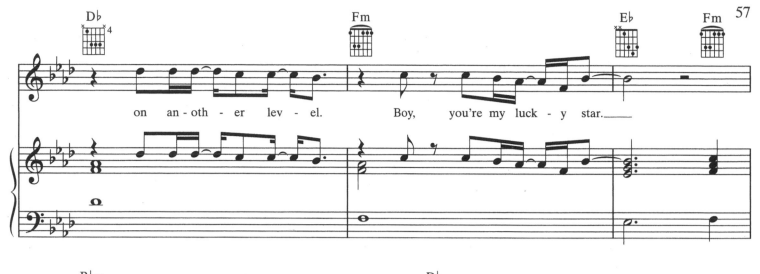

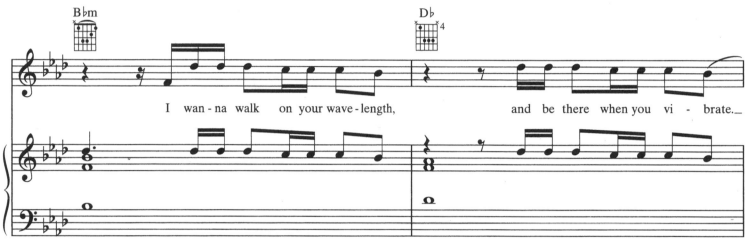

Ex - tra - ter - res - tri - al.____

Ex - tra - ter - res - tri - al.____ Boy, you're an a - li - en,___

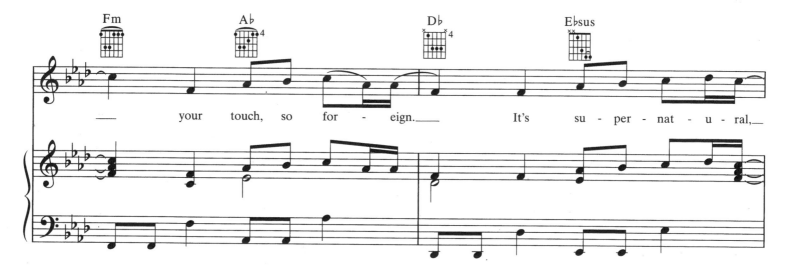

___ your touch, so for - eign.____ It's su - per - nat - u - ral,___

___ ex - tra - ter - res - tri - al._____

# WHO AM I LIVING FOR?

Words and Music by
KATY PERRY, CHRISTOPHER STEWART,
THOMAS BRIAN and MONTE NEUBLE

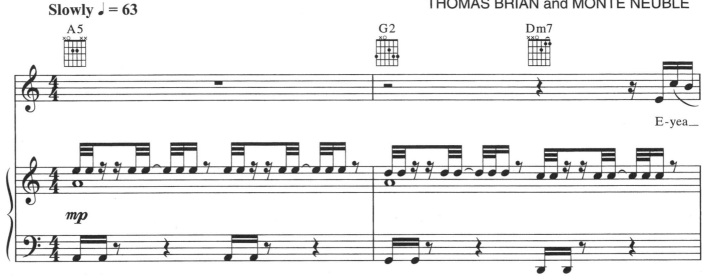

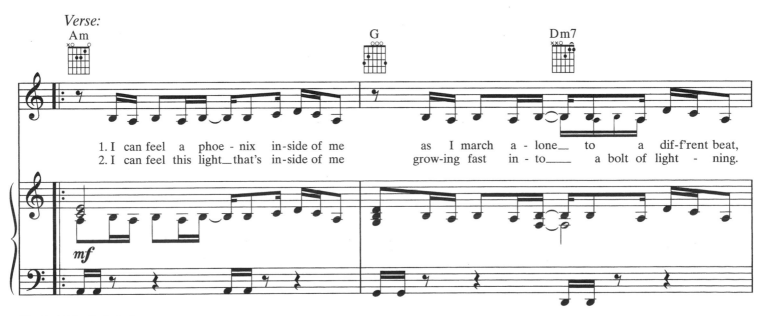

Who Am I Living For? - 5 - 1

I can see the heav-ens, but I still hear the flames call — ing out my na — ame.

**% Chorus:**

I can see the writ - ing on the wall.___ I can't ig - nore this war.___

**1.**

At the end___ of it all,___ who am I liv - ing for?___

**2.3.**

___ who am I liv - ing for?___

Heav-y is the head that wears the crown.\_ Don't let the great - ness get you down.

*D.S. 𝄋 al Coda*

Heav-y is the head that wears the crown.\_ Don't let the great - ness get you down. Oh,_____ yeah.

⊕ *Coda*

At the end, at the end. Who am I liv - ing for?\_\_\_\_\_

# PEARL

Words and Music by
KATY PERRY, CHRISTOPHER STEWART
and GREG WELLS

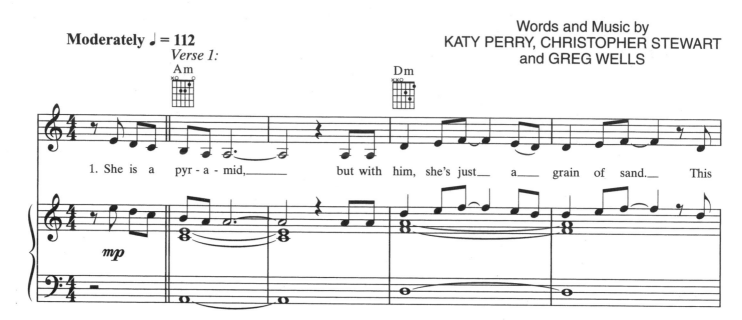

1. She is a pyr-a-mid,_____ but with him, she's just__ a__ grain of sand.__ This

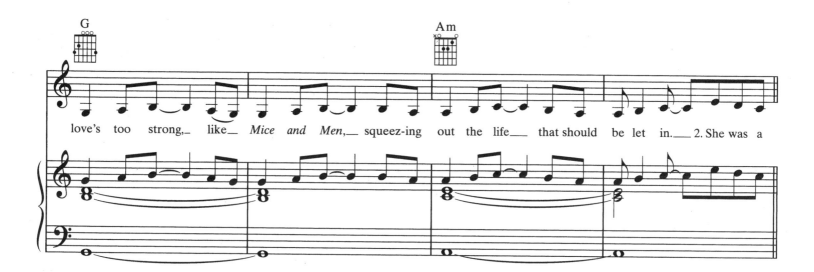

love's too strong,__ like *Mice and Men,*__ squeez-ing out the life__ that should be let in.__ 2. She was a

hur-ri-cane-cane-cane-cane,
stop-pa-ble,

but now, she's just__ a__ gust of wind.__ She used to
move fast just like__ an__ av-a-lanche.__ But

set the sails___ of a thou-sand ships,___ was a force___ to___ be reck-oned with.___
now she's stuck___ deep in ce-ment,___ wish-ing that they nev-er,___ ev-er met.___

She could be___ a Stat-ue of Lib-er-ty. She could be___ a Joan of Arc.___

But he's scared___ of the light that's in-side of her, so he keeps her in the dark.___

𝄋 *Chorus:*

1. 2. Oh, she used to be a pearl.___ Oh.___
3. You don't have to be a shell,___ no.___

# HUMMINGBIRD HEARTBEAT

Words and Music by
KATY PERRY, CHRISTOPHER STEWART,
STACY BARTHE and MONTE NEUBLE

1. You make me feel like I'm los-ing my vir-gin-i-ty.__ The first time, ev-'ry

2. I've flown a mil-lion miles__ just to find a mag-ic seed,__ a wild flow-er with the

time when you're touch-ing me. I'll make you bloom like a flow-er that you've nev-er seen.

pow-er to bring life to me. You're so ex-ot-ic, get my whole__ bod-y flut-ter-ing,

*Original recording in F# major.

Hummingbird Heartbeat - 5 - 1

# NOT LIKE THE MOVIES

Words and Music by
KATY PERRY and GREG WELLS

Verse 1 (sing 1st time only):

1. He put it on___ me, I put it on,___ like there was noth-ing

Verse 2 (sing 2nd time only):

2. Snow White said when I was young,___ "One day my prince will

wrong. It did-n't fit,___ it was-n't right,___ was-n't just the size. They say you know when you

come." So I wait for that date. They say it's hard to meet your

*2nd time, piano 8<sup>vb</sup>.

Not Like the Movies - 6 - 1

dream - ing___ that I___ could?___

___ he'll be the one that fin - ish - es your sen - tenc - es.___

*Chorus:*

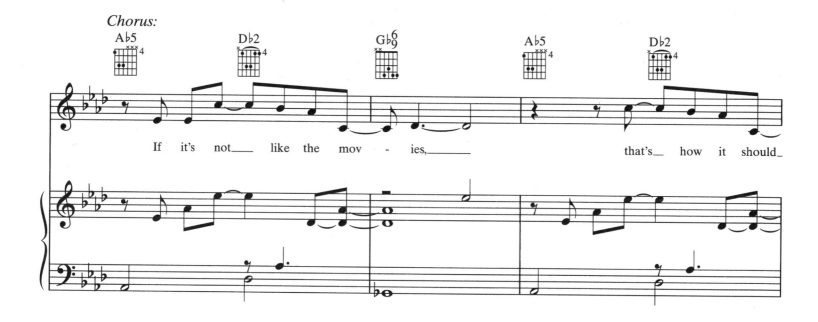

If it's not___ like the mov - ies,___ that's___ how it should_

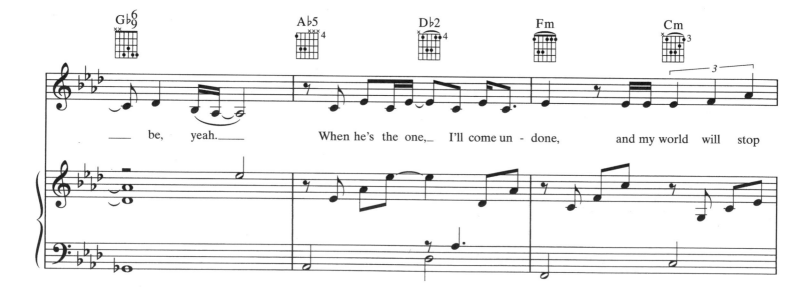

___ be, yeah.___ When he's the one,_ I'll come un - done, and my world will stop